shape and space without a worksheet

for Reception and Year 1

Early Childhood Mathematics Group

Introduction

The Early Childhood Mathematics Group is one of ATM's working groups. It started in 1996 and meets twice a term in London at the Institute of Education in Bedford Way, W1.

The members of the group are practitioners working in the foundation stage, mathematics education lecturers, local education advisors, consultants, teachers and those interested in early years' education issues as they relate to the teaching and learning of mathematics. We share problems and solutions and look at the realities of classroom practice. We also take on tasks such as writing responses to curriculum documents, writing articles for professional publications and developing curriculum materials.

This book has been written as a companion book to previous ATM publications, **Number without a worksheet** and **Exploring mathematics with younger children**. We hope that the practical activities suggested will encourage teachers and classroom assistants to work with young children to enhance their mathematical thinking and communication skills while engaged in meaningful, enjoyable activities.

Authors from **The Early Childhood Mathematics Group**:

Pam Baldwin
Grace Cook
Sheila Ebbutt
Sue Gifford
Marjorie Gorman
Pauline Hoare
Jean Millar
Val Shaw
Mary Southall
Romey Tacon

Equipment

- Poleidoblocs
- Logiblocs
- Cuisinaire
- ATM Mathematical Activity Tiles
- Polydron and Clixi
- 3D shapes, including lots of irregular shapes
- 2D shapes, including lots of irregular shapes
- Community Playthings blocks
- a variety of mirrors (bubble, concave, distortion, box, tray, cube, prism…)
- Pixie, Roamer, BeeBot

Design: DCG Design, Cambridge

Illustrations: **Tamaris Taylor**

Activities

1 Journeys

Mathematical learning

Position, direction, sequence

Resources

Rosie's Walk by Pat Hutchins

The Bear Hunt by Michael Rose

CD of *The Bear Hunt* with sound and rhythm

The Train Ride by June Crebbin

Small world, play mats, construction

Main activity

Sit together on a carpet. Tell or read the story. Use a story map. You could use a large floor map with characters from the story.

Children then draw or build their own story map with blocks and use appropriate characters to tell the story.

Children draw one part of the story.

Children bring all this back to the carpet activity.

Extensions

Create your own journey in the garden. Take a sack to collect items as you go.

Recreate the journey in the sand tray.

Play the story tape or CD.

Build/draw/chalk a story map on playground. Paint the map with water on the ground. Place collected items on the map.

Simplification

Make a track/pathway that will send the traveller into and out of a tunnel, over and under bridges

Questions

- Recall: Where did children go after the deep cold river?

- Can you draw a plan? Can you show on your plan which way they went?

- How can you tell your friend how to go from one place to another if the start and end positions are given. (How do you get from a to b?)

Variation

Use Pixie (Roamer, BeeBot) and a play mat.

Outdoors

Repeat the activity with the children as the story characters.

Recording suggestion

Use a digital camera to show real journeys or to create a map.

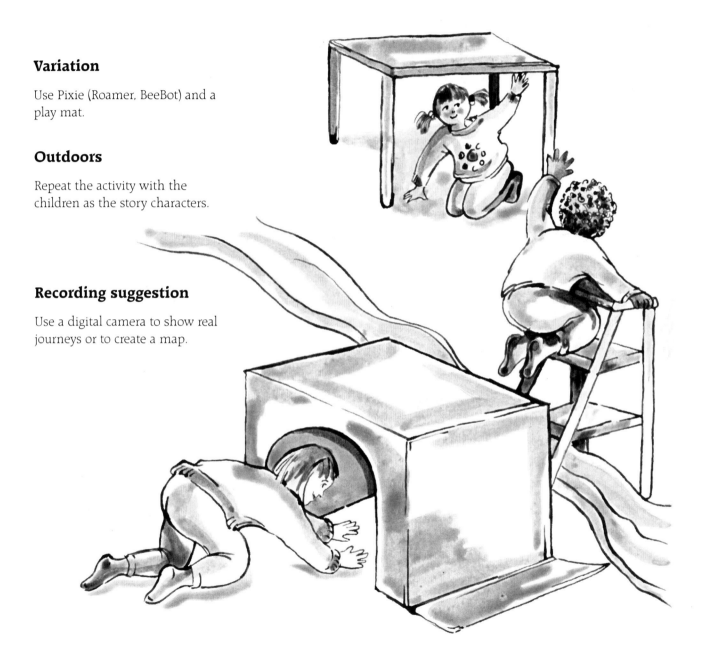

2 Pretending

Mathematical learning

Visualising, predicting

Recognising and describing position

Properties of 2D and 3D shapes

Resources

Stories like *Tom Thumb*, *The Borrowers*, *Mrs Pepperpot*

Boxes large and small

Smartie tube and match box

Large caterpillar tube

Outdoor climbing apparatus

Jack-in-the-box

Guatamalan dream dolls in a tiny box

Main activity

In the outdoor area explore the apparatus that you climb into. Or use a large portable caterpillar tube and huge cardboard boxes. Ask children what they see and feel above them and behind and round them.

Read or tell one of the stories to the group. Ask the children to pretend they are the same size as the characters in the story, and they walk into a large empty Smartie tube lying along the ground.

At the end of the activity, go on to the real apparatus again and talk to children about whether it was as they imagined it.

Questions

- What can you see in front of you? What is behind you?

- What can you feel if you put out your hands to the sides?

- Would the sides be flat or curved?

- What if you were to lie down?

Extension

Away from the apparatus, invite children to mime feeling the walls of the box or tube round them. Ask them to imagine they are inside a box and they are feeling all the walls above, below, in front, and behind.

Simplification

Work on the real apparatus and discuss with children what they are actually seeing and feeling.

Recording suggestion

Encourage children to describe their imagined views on tape, or try to draw them.

3 Tangrams

Mathematical learning

Properties of 2D shapes

Naming 2D shapes

Describing irregular shapes

Position, movement

Resources

A large supply of coloured card squares, cut as shown.

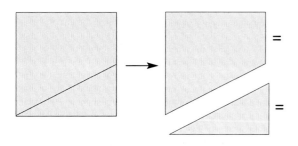

Display paper, glue

Main activity

Children work with a partner to make different shapes using the pieces.

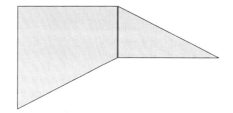

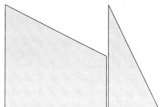

Questions

- What shapes have you found?
- How are these shapes the same and how they are different?
- Can you make another shape like this?
- Have we found all the different shapes?
- How do you know?
- What happens if we turn this shape?
- Does it look like this?
- How would you describe your shape? What does it look like?

Extension

Children use a tangram with three pieces

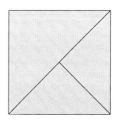

Simplification

Make the shapes larger.

8

Variation

Exploding shapes: Give each child two squares of gummed paper (or card and glue), one square to be cut into several pieces. Arrange the cut pieces on a background of sugar paper so it appears that the shape has 'exploded'.

Ask children to compare the original and exploded shapes - how are they the same, how are they different?

Outdoors

Use large card tangrams or carpet tile shapes.

Chalk outlines of shapes like the ones made by the children.

Children play games where they run to particular shapes according to instructions. For example:

   Run to the shape with three corners

   Walk to the shape with four straight sides

   Hop to the triangle shape

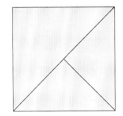
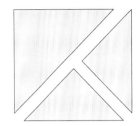

Recording Suggestion

Children record their new shapes by sticking them on paper, drawing round them or copying onto paper.

4 A Construction Site

Mathematical learning

Describing 3D shapes

Fitting shapes together

Matching shapes

Building up shapes

Resources

empty boxes of various shapes and sizes

cardboard boxes filled with screwed-up newspaper to strengthen them, and sealed with tape

Community Playthings blocks

Poleidoblocs

hard hats, clipboards

real bricks

building plans

pictures of buildings

Main activity

Children use boxes or blocks to create a building site. Allow time for sustained development of tasks and role-play.

Encourage children to talk about the activity and describe the 'buildings' being developed.

Simplification

Free play with blocks or boxes.

Questions

- How can you carry a lot of bricks at the same time?
- How can you make this wall longer /wider/ higher?
- How can you make the tower taller?
- What shape are the windows? The doors?
- What shape have you used for the roof?
- What shape would fit in this space?
- What if you turned the shape round?

Variation

Children use table-top equipment such as Poleidoblocs or create a building site in the sand tray, using small construction toys.

Extensions

Build a tall tower. Stand on a table and look down on it. What can you see? What can't you see?

When 'the building site' theme is 'worked out' have a 'demolition' company to come and clear the site. Examine the 'debris' left by the demolition contractors. Point out that useful materials should be re-cycled. Ask children:

How could we use these materials again?

Where can these shapes be stored?

Which shapes can be stacked?

Which shapes do not stack?

Outdoors

Children use large play equipment with pieces of wood for ramps etc

Recording suggestion

Encourage children to record developments by drawing, or taking digital photographs as play progresses.

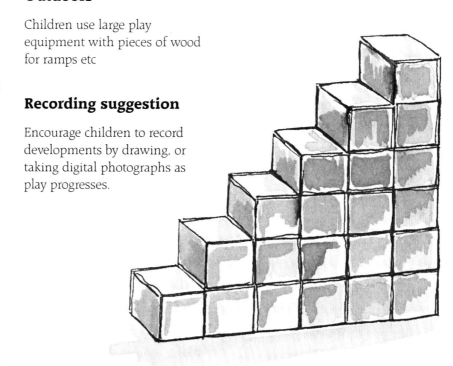

5 Irregular Shape Bingo

Mathematical learning

Properties of irregular 2D shapes

Extending mathematical language

Resources

6–12 non-standard shapes in stiff cardboard (for example, sets of 'nearly' circles, or 'nearly' triangles, or 'nearly' rectangles)

Bingo boards – each different – one for each child

Main activity

Show each shape in turn and ask children to say what it looks like. Keep turning the shape as you go round the group, encouraging each child to say something different about it, such as 'It's a doughnut' or 'It's a moon' or 'It's roundy with a bit missing'. (Make a note of their descriptions.)

Give each child a bingo board. Hide the shapes and secretly choose one at a time. Using the children's descriptions, ask,

'Who's got the doughnut?' 'Who's got round shape with the bit missing?'

The child who has the shape on the board wins the shape.

Continue until all the boards are complete.

Simplification

Use only 3 shapes – each child has the same shapes in different orientations.

Extensions

Children sort a collection of irregular off cuts of card. Give each child a handful to sort and ask them to give reasons for their selection.

Collect 'nearly' shapes.

Questions

- What do you notice about this shape?
- What else can you say about it?
- Can you see another shape that's a bit like this one?

Variation

Repeat the activity for irregular 3D shapes. Use photographs of interesting shapes, taken with a digital camera.

Recording Suggestions

Children stick down their own collection of off-cuts and say why they have put those shapes together.

Children sort out the shapes according to a chosen property.

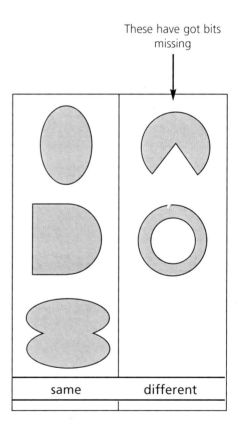

These have got bits missing

13

6 Using the Environment

Mathematical learning

Naming and properties of shapes

Position

Recognising shapes that are nearly the same

Resources

Sets of mathematical 2D and 3D shapes

Photographs

Digital camera

Main activity

The group sits in a circle. Place a range of 2D and 3D shapes in the centre. Ask children to look at the shapes carefully and then to look around to find something that is the same shape or nearly the same shape. Ask, 'what can you see around you that is the same, or similar to a shape in the circle?'

Provide individual clipboards with a shape in a tray. Children walk around the classroom or garden to find shapes that are the same or similar to the shape on the tray. Children use the clipboard to record their findings.

Extensions

Create an interactive display that children can add to. Shapes can be from home. Talk about the shapes they have brought.

Children make prints using paint and plastic 3D shapes. Ask:

How many different shapes can you print from each shape?

Have you found all the possible shapes?

How do you know?

Use photo-posters of buildings. Children take 2D or 3D shapes from a feely bag and match them to the shapes on different parts of the photos of buildings.

Simplification

Children make a shape from play dough to match the one in the middle of the table.

Questions

- What can you see that is the same /similar?
- Why you have chosen this?
- How are they the same?
- How are they different?

Recording suggestions

Add labels to the shape display explaining why it was selected for the display.

Display a photo of a building and link 2D or 3D shapes to it with ribbons.

7 What do you see?

Mathematical learning

Properties of 2D and 3D shapes

Naming shapes

Describing shapes

Extending mathematical language

Resources

Feely bag

Screen

Selection of regular and irregular 2D and 3D shapes

Main activity

Start with the group sitting on the carpet. Have a selection of shapes (2D or 3D) in a 'feely' bag that is passed round the group. Children take turns to take a shape from the bag and describe its attributes. Encourage correct use of language and provide the name of the shape.

Extension

Use a Screen – a hard-back book is useful. Have a selection of shapes hidden behind it. Show a small part of the shape and ask children to name the shape.

Questions

- What can you see?
- How do you know?
- Could it be a triangle?
- Could it be a square? Gradually reveal more until the children are certain.

Simplification

Children take shapes from a feely bag and match them to similar shapes in the middle of the table.

Variation

Children work in pairs. One child shows shapes from behind a screen; the partner has to describe and name the shapes.

Recording suggestions

Encourage the children to choose one shape and draw a picture using only that shape. Supply children with circular paper and circles of different sizes to glue on to paper or card to make a circle picture.

Main activity

Set up a maze outside using large equipment (a frame, tunnels, planks, slides etc). Children decide with a friend which pathway to choose and try it out. They direct each other round the obstacles, using instructions such as

Take three steps forward. Take two steps to the left.

Encourage children to talk about their chosen pathways.

Extensions

Children build mazes from empty boxes or construction materials within a tray or photocopy paper box lid.

Make a Lego maze on a Lego baseboard. Roll a marble through it.

Simplification

Ask children to find a pathway with a friend around the objects – free play.

Questions

- How did you find your way through the maze?
- What shapes did you see?
- Did you go under any shapes?
- What did you have to go through?

Variation

Set up a similar maze indoors. Children choose their own pathways.

Recording suggestion

Encourage children to record their paths through the maze by drawings.

Mathematical learning

Position, direction and movement,

Experiencing turning left, right, finding a pathway

Resources

Construction toys

Empty boxes (cuboids)

Xerox paper boxes and lids

Mazes book

Making a maze in the snow

Book 'Not now Bernard' – (re-contextualised into a maze)

The story of the Minotaur and Ariadne's ball of string

9 Body shapes

Mathematical learning

Symmetry

Different shapes

Describing properties of shape and movements

Developing vocabulary for describing shapes

Resources

Children themselves

Dance music

Main activity

Children move around where there is space and follow suggestions for changing their bodies into different shapes. Use a range of mathematical terms and comparatives such as round, rounder, long, longer, and opposites such as long, short, high, low, under, over, left and right.

Encourage children to use their arms when balancing and become aware of the natural symmetrical arrangement of parts of the body.

Children move to music or the rhythm of a percussion instrument.

Extension

Firework dances – Children make movements and shapes to represent different fireworks.

Simplification

Children make one large circle by holding hands. Arrange a simple dance by making steps to the right, steps to the left, moving into the centre and back.

Questions

- What did you notice when we made shapes?
- How did you make a taller/ shorter shape?
- Which firework did you pretend to be?
- Could you go as high as the firework?

Variation

Children work in pairs. One does a simple dance. The partner acts as the 'mirror' and reflects the movements. Then, they change roles.

Recording suggestions

Replay the music. Children make drawings on large sheets of paper with a crayon in each hand to replicate the movements they made.

Children record the dances in their own way.

Talk about what they did in a tape recorder.

Record activities using a digital camera.

Mirrors 10

Main activity

Work with a small group of children to explore the pictures in the magic mirror books. Demonstrate how moving the mirror helps to complete the pictures. Show how the mirror is along the line of symmetry when they can see the 'whole' picture.

Children work in pairs with mirrors and collections of shapes. Include semicircles and right-angled triangles so they can make circles, squares and rectangles when using the mirrors.

[Use the shapes at the back of this book to be changed with the mirrors.]

Extensions

Make hinged mirrors by taping two mirrors together to give a kaleidoscope effect.

Children place shapes between the mirrors and describe what they can see.

Look at distorting mirrors.

Draw a picture of yourself in a spoon or a saucepan.

Simplification

Children investigate mirror books for themselves.

Questions

- What do you see in the mirrors?
- What happens when you move the mirrors?
- What happens when you move the object in front of the mirror?
- What happens when you move the shape nearer the mirror, or further away?
- How does your face change if you draw it looking in a spoon?

Variation

Large mirrors, mounted on walls, floors and ceilings, are much favoured in Reggio Emilia nurseries to provide stimulus to children to talk about images, shapes and reflections of objects and themselves.

Recording suggestion

Encourage children to talk about and draw what they see.

Mathematical learning

Symmetry

Properties of shapes

Position and movement

Resources

Magic Mirror Books Marian Walter

Hinged mirrors

Small plastic mirrors

Kaleidoscopes

Reggio Emilia mirrors

Mirror boxes, concave and convex mirrors, distorting mirrors

Spoons, saucepans, and other reflective surfaces

11 Folding

Mathematical learning

Symmetry

Properties of shapes

Position and movement

Resources

Large tablecloth

J cloths, calico squares, paper napkins, kitchen roll, felt shapes

Main activity

A small group of children, about six, sit in a circle. Have an unfolded tablecloth in a bag. Ask children to take the cloth from the bag and spread it out flat. Ask them to first walk around, then across the tablecloth.

Ask:

What shape is the cloth?

How can you turn it into another shape?

Children use their own piece of fabric or a paper napkin to make their own new shapes and then describe them.

Extension

Provide different fabric shapes and challenge the children to make other shapes.

Simplification

Use plain A4 paper. Fold the paper in any way three times, squash the folds, open it up and talk about the shapes that can be seen.

Questions

- How many different shapes can you make with just one fold?

- How many shapes using two folds?

Variations

Fold A4 paper to make a square by tearing or cutting.

Make little booklets.

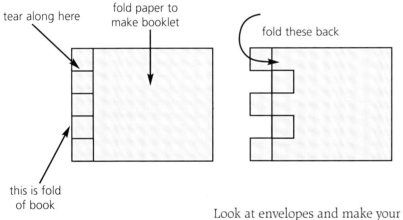

Look at envelopes and make your own.

Make zigzag books.

Do simple paper engineering.

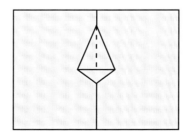

Make simple paper boats, hats and boxes by folding.

Make paper aeroplanes and helicopters.

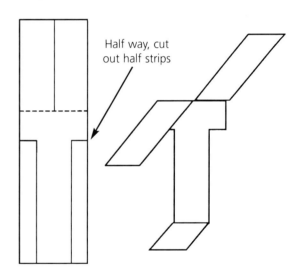

Outdoors

In the garden, use a parachute or a huge blanket.

Recording suggestion

Encourage the children to draw the shapes as they fold.

12 Covering

Mathematial learning

Properties of 2D and 3D shapes

Visualising

Resources

Stories: My Cat likes to hide in boxes, Bugs in a box, Wayne's Shape

Empty boxes (of various shapes and sizes)

Plain paper, wrapping paper, newspaper, tin foil, tissue paper, bubble wrap, brown paper, sticky tape, masking tape, PVA glue, Pritt stick

IKEA nesting boxes

Main activity

Empty boxes opened up and flattened out. Fold again, inside out and join with tape.

Children choose paper to wrap their 'present'.

Decorate the paper with other collage materials.

Extension

When the box is flattened, draw round the net onto wrapping paper.

Simplification

Children wrap boxes that have not been opened up.

Questions

- What shape is your box?

- What do you think was inside this box?

- What shapes can you see when you open your box?

- How much paper do you need to wrap your box?

- What if your paper isn't big enough to wrap your box?

- If you were to send your box in the post, would it arrive in one piece?

Variations

Can you make or find a set of boxes that fit inside each other?

Write numbers on the boxes. Ask children to put that number of things in the box.

Fill boxes with multilink, unifix, cubes, pasta etc. Ask: How many pieces will fit into each box?

Out doors

Covering big boxes and other equipment with tablecloths and or fabric.

Covering buildings (in your imagination).

How much paper will we need to wrap the school? (Link into Christmas).

Recording suggestion

Children record by using digital cameras.

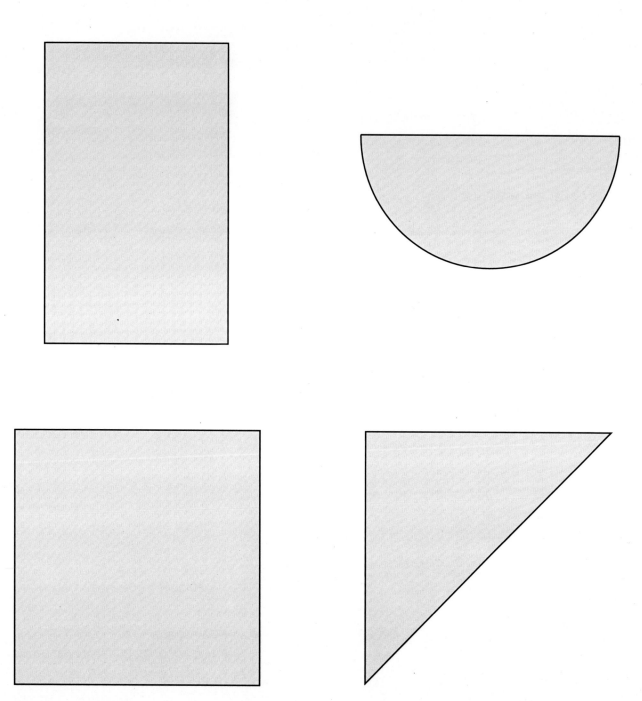